Pandemic

POEMS

OTHER BOOKS BY
PHILIP RESNICK

MEMOIR

Itineraries: An Intellectual Odyssey (2020)

NON-FICTION

The Land of Cain (1977)

Parliament vs. People (1984)

Letters to a Québécois Friend (1990)

*The Masks of Proteus: Canadian
Reflections on the State* (1990)

Toward a Canada-Quebec Union (1991)

Thinking English Canada (1994)

Twenty-First Century Democracy (1997)

*The Politics of Resentment: British Columbia
Regionalism and Canadian Unity* (2000)

The European Roots of Canadian Identity (2005)

The Labyrinth of North American Identities (2012)

POETRY

Between Two Holocausts (1962)

Poems for Andromache (1975)

Poems of Pelion (1979)

The Centaur's Mountain (1986)

Footsteps of the Past (2015)

Passageways (2018)

Pandemic
POEMS

Philip Resnick

RONSDALE

RONSDALE PRESS
3350 West 21st Avenue
Vancouver, B.C., Canada V6S 1G7
www.ronsdalepress.com

Typesetting: Julie Cochrane, in New Baskerville 11 pt on 13.5
Cover Design: Julie Cochrane
Paper: Enviro 100 Edition, 60 lb. Natural Cream (FSC) —
    100% post-consumer waste, totally chlorine-free and acid-free

Ronsdale Press wishes to thank the following for their support of its publishing program: the Canada Council for the Arts, the Government of Canada, the British Columbia Arts Council, and the Province of British Columbia through the Book Publishing Tax Credit Program.

Library and Archives Canada Cataloguing in Publication

Title: Pandemic poems / Philip Resnick.
Names: Resnick, Philip, author.
Description: First edition.
Identifiers: Canadiana (print) 20210194499 | Canadiana (ebook) 20210194545 | ISBN 9781553806448 (softcover) | ISBN 9781553806455 (ebook) | ISBN 9781553806462 (PDF)
Subjects: LCSH: COVID-19 Pandemic, 2020—Poetry.
Classification: LCC PS8585.E8 P36 2021 | DDC C811/.54—dc23

At Ronsdale Press we are committed to protecting the environment. To this end we are working with Canopy and printers to phase out our use of paper produced from ancient forests. This book is one step towards that goal.

Printed in Canada by Island Blue, Victoria, B.C.

to all who have had to endure
the trials and tribulations of the
COVID-19 pandemic

ACKNOWLEDGEMENTS

Selected poems from this collection were first published in Issues 47 and 48 of the online journal *Inroads.*

"Of Muses," was published in the April, 2021 issue of *The Literary Review of Canada*

CONTENTS

To the reader,

On New Year's Day, 2020, I scribbled a short poem anticipating the start of a new decade. Though fires were raging through the Austral bush, we living in the northern hemisphere, despite the ever-growing dangers of climate change, could still look forward to the approaching year with modest confidence.

In my case, there would be a memoir, entitled *Itineraries: An Intellectual Odyssey*, to be published in the spring, followed by several months that summer in the house by the Aegean, inherited from my late wife's grandfather, in Damoukhari, a lovely cove at the bottom of Mount Pelion.

Like the rest of us, my life changed abruptly from mid-March on. What had seemed a far-off episode of zoonotic transfer in a wet market in Wuhan had quickly become a global pandemic, forcing country after country to close down, and bringing the global economy and day to day patterns of life to a halt.

Book launches of the traditional sort became a thing of the past, travel overseas as well, as I too found myself increasingly living in confinement. This in a city, Vancouver, with enough greenery, forest trails, and seawalls, to make the new dispensation more bearable.

Strangely, I began to find inspiration of a sort in the crisis now upon us. It is as though I had a pandemic muse by my shoulder, whispering themes and lines as the weeks and months unfolded.

What follows is my version of *A Journal of the Plague Year*, to borrow the title of Daniel Defoe's account of the Great Plague of London of 1665. But mine would take the form of poetry, not prose, and would be written during the first pandemic year of COVID-19, rather than fifty years after the event.

Most of the poems in this collection, not surprisingly, are downbeat in tone. For a tragic element has entered our collective lives, one which the lucky generation of which I was a part had never experienced before. The pandemic would be as much of a wake-up call for us as the two World Wars or the Great Depression would have been for the generations that preceded.

I offer these poems to the reader as the reflections of someone who has tried to make sense of the challenge that has turned the world we had known until now upside down.

Philip Resnick
Vancouver, March 2021

COVID-19

Plague has always had a fascination
for those who map the subterranean, the macabre,
black bile overflowing, feverish gaze,
bloated corpses, tumbrels rolling through medieval towns,
death in Venice,
love in the age of cholera.
So it is with the coronavirus,
spreading its bat-like wings across the planet,
transforming species that had become our prey
into avenging angels,
hugging the elderly to their chests,
surfacing where least expected,
turning the global economy topsy-turvy
and the best-laid plans of empire builders
into crumbling sand.

Feb. 28

The End of Time

For centuries old Believers prostrated themselves,
lacerating flesh and entrails,
convinced the great upheaval around them
had some higher purpose,
that out of chaos and destruction a New Jerusalem,
for those who had abjured their sins,
would ultimately emerge.
Subsequently, as traditional beliefs were cast aside,
new credos arose with their adherents,
having beheaded kings and overthrown czars,
certain a new age could begin
and humanity shed the vices
petrified by ignorance and accumulated privilege.
Now that such beliefs have also bitten the dust,
seers amongst us and myriads who live in fear,
sense climate wars, droughts, and pestilence
foreshadowing the end of time.

March 19

Globalization's Children

"We others, civilizations,
now know that we are mortal."
— Paul Valery, 1919

It seemed obvious enough,
for those who has bloodied themselves in the trenches,
seen the swathe of carnage
bell towers and market squares had endured
and millions dying from the accursed flu,
as though a vengeful god
were calling in a sinful continent's debts.
What about us, globalization's children,
spared the previous century's major wars,
wearing our affluence like a fashion statement
from a new-age couturier,
convinced the arrow would always point upwards,
that the merry-go-round would never stop
for us lucky ones who'd managed to embark.

March 23

Slow Time

When the pandemic will have felled its final victim
— a geriatric with an underlying heart condition
or a child in a torpid refugee camp —
and the epidemiologists and public health officials
with their grim recitations of the daily toll
will have beaten a retreat
as a more frenetic pace of life resumes,
what will we have learned
from the weeks and months of our confinement?
That the days are long and the nights even longer
when we cannot punctuate them with the din and glitter
of the bar scene, the theatres and sports arenas,
our all-important lunch dates and dinner rendez-vous,
the endless meetings and projects to keep us on our toes,
the trips back east, out west, and overseas
for we are a restless bunch always on the move,
the cruise ships for those insane enough
to tempt the fates again?
What we may have to show
are like those intimate diaries that never seem to end,
the meals we forced ourselves to cook,
as though it matters what we ate or drank,
the endless phone conversations, Netflix,
and sorties on the Web,
the wrangling with the kids,
the sexual act as a form of penance or relief,
the strange compulsion to explore
our inner doubts and long-time fantasies
now that the doors were locked
and there was no escaping.

March 24

On a Passage in Lenin

"There are decades when nothing happens,
and there are weeks when decades happen."
— Vladimir Lenin

True enough where revolutions are concerned,
the French, the Russian for starters.
No less true for financial crises,
1929, 2008, to name two of the biggies.
Plagues too have had their cataclysmic high points,
the Bubonic Plague, the Columbian exchange, the Spanish flu.
Still early days for the coronavirus,
no seers at the city gates able to foretell
just how it will evolve or peak,
how much of the societal carapace will remain intact.
But we sense,
much like barn animals before a hurricane or tsunami,
that this is the real thing,
that somewhere in mid-March
the earth turned on its axis
and those who lived through it
will never be the same.

March 25

Contagion

"Of what use is the past?" the moderns asked,
secure in the comforts of the present-day
and the promise of a future still at hand.
"Of what use the aged," the millennials chimed in,
"they who have enjoyed the earth's fruits these many years,
and refuse to clear the way for those now come of age?"
"Of what use the homeless and the poor,"
the well-off complained,
"they who spread vermin in their clothes and hair
while we must take shelter behind the ramparts of our homes?"
"Of what use your pristine beaches and winter holidays,"
the ascetics railed,
"when the pillars of your temples and pleasure palaces
have come crashing down?"
"Of what use your lamentations?" the sybarites replied,
"let us drink and eat and copulate our fill
while we party through the night."

March 26

Fear

You see it in their faces,
in the quick manoeuvres to step aside
on sidewalks and on trails,
in the panicked emails,
the endless stories in the papers
or posted on the Web.
Pandora's box has been pried open,
spectres one had thought wrestled to the ground
by science, research, and biotech
haunt the deserted boardrooms and chancelleries
from one OECD capital to the next.
Half the planet has gone into hibernation,
even as the other half, the poorer half,
awaits its turn,
hospital wards already overflowing
with the prostate, the skeletal, the breathless.
Through the ages, fear has worn many masks,
conquering armies, devastating famines,
despots doing in their subjects with a mere flick of the wrist,
but its most primal form as always
remains the fear of death.

March 27

Nemesis

There had been intonations of a bubbly stock exchange,
target cities — Venice, Barcelona, Amsterdam —
besieged by tourist crowds,
cruise ships too big to dock,
real estate markets too frothy for mere proles.
The game seemed so humongous it would never cease,
the moneyed folks too powerful to fail,
their chains of command spanning continents and seas,
dwarfing nation-states along the way.
True, climate change frayed at the edges,
a host of civil wars raged on,
fraught refugees and asylum seekers
vying for a brief fifteen minutes in the sun.
So when the virus made its first appearance
in the then little-known city of Wuhan,
it seemed a minor nuisance,
a freakish zoonotic passage from bats to humankind.
The rest is history
as the global skein unravelled,
Nemesis, vengeful goddess,
stirring from the depths,
the global circus careening to a crash.

March 28

Meltdown

Two weeks since the lockdown, the social distancing,
began in earnest,
living at close quarters with her parents,
severed from friends, school,
the little interactions and the big that matter,
an adolescent after all,
having to listen incessantly to her mom,
"Do this, maybe you shouldn't do that,"
her very tone offensive,
her body language even more so,
beginning to drive her mad.
So here on the Pacific Spirit Park trail
where countless locked-in city folk
come to decompress this Sunday morning
she lets fly her bottled-up rage,
a sign perhaps
of where well-mannered Vancouverites
may be headed.

March 30

Of Guelfs and Ghibellines

"They were fiercely hostile to me and to my ancestors
and to my party, so that twice I scattered them."
— Inferno, x, 46–48

Dante, journeying through the Inferno,
encounters shades of the Guelf-Ghibelline rivalry,
of bloody feuds and battles,
leading to exile that rankles even after death.
To this day Sienese fans at football matches
taunt the Florentines,
who lost 4000 at the 1260 battle of Montaperti,
by chanting "Montaperti, Montaperti."
And we wonder why Sunnis and Shiites
despise each other with such fervour
much like secular Israelis, Haredim,
why Hindu mobs scourge Muslims
and the Irish proved unforgiving in their hatreds,
why Reds hate Blues in the USA
with a passion that even plague will not diminish.

March 31

Inspired in part by Prue Shaw, *Reading Dante: From Here to Eternity*

A Human Face

If there is a human face
to the calamity sweeping across the globe
it is not the well-heeled retirees
or other denizens of first world opulence
stuck on cruise ships
or in trophy tourist destinations far from home.
Nor even the rickety aged,
suffering from dementia and assorted chronic illnesses
in first world nursing homes
where the virus can find easy prey.
It is Zakir Hussain and millions like him
in third world shanty towns, improvised shelters,
and overflowing refugee camps,
living testimony to our planet's callousness.

April 1

Man and Society in Calamity

Decades ago in the library at Sciences Po,
I recall perusing Sorokin's World War II vintage volume
with a foreboding title,
overwhelmed by its encyclopedic range and power.
Faithful to his Russian roots,
his apocalyptical disposition,
he mapped state institutions through the millennia,
advancing wherever plague, famine, war or revolution
scorched the earth and singed the heavens.
In the troubled times we now encounter
it feels as though an old world prophet
had foreseen back then how a mutated virus
could hone in on a perfect target,
shredding an epoch's shared illusions
in the process.

April 2

Pitrim Sorokin, *Man and Society in Calamity*, 1942

The Lucky Generation

We called ourselves the lucky generation,
in many ways we were,
spared the wars, the dole,
the diseases, the back-breaking toil,
that has been our predecessors' lot
and that of the myriads who had come before them.
There was comfort in knowing we could choose
which college to enrol in,
which profession we might enter,
what city or country to put roots down in,
where we might holiday winter or summer
or retire to when our working lives were over.
There were passing clouds in the sky,
Islamist disruptions here and there,
the occasional economic downturn,
hints of glaciers melting or sea levels rising,
but for the large part these were problems
the millennials and their offspring would have to bear.
And suddenly we learned how quickly
the script could be rewritten,
carefully constructed stage sets taken down,
the myths of exponential growth,
globalization as some kind of magic key,
affluence as a guarantee of personal immunity,
reduced to tatters.
The old Greek precept which Solon had first uttered
had stood the test of time:
"Do not count yourself fortunate until your final day."

April 4

The Muse

My favourite muse, Erato,
has instructed me in no uncertain terms,
to lay off the virus for a while.
"Enough gloom and doom," she says,
"find some more cheerful themes,
the cherry blossoms in full bloom,
the magnolia buds,
the daffodils piercing through the ground.
Or try the rites of spring,
the mating geese and ducks,
the herons in their nests by Stanley Park,
the young couples hiving off the beaten trail."
And then she adds with faltering voice,
"Our oldest sister, Melpomene,
has come down with the dreaded bug."

April 6

Life Storm

Schubert Lebensstürme,
performed by Lucas and Arthur Jussen

In his short life,
Schubert managed to span half a musical world
with his *Lieder,* his *Fantasie,* his piano trios and symphonies,
and his *Lebensstürme.*
So ably played by this young Dutch duo,
it captures the high points and the low
of what entraps us
from our first breath to our last.
In a season when the plague
has set its banner so firmly in our midst
and the news is about isolation, desolation, and despair,
one cherishes how the Jussens wrestle with the storm.

April 10

The Deck

Fir and west coast cedar lurch skywards
in the woods across,
next door a magnolia blooms,
as a skill saw a few doors down
cuts boards for a back-yard project.
A surfeit of neighbours for a mid-week afternoon,
but the spring air is feverish with promise
and the dog-days of summer still months ahead.
To shut one's eyes, albeit for a few instants,
is to forget the merciless refrain
with which media and Web compound an epidemic
into an end-of-the-world moment,
to escape as best one can
into whatever inner shelter one can construct
within the finite confines of a simple deck.

April 13

Confinement

Half the planet, including its perennial high-flyers,
has, courtesy of the spiked intruder,
discovered the fine points of social distancing,
of living in a closed space, 23/24 on 7,
even as the sun is warming up the earth,
the trees and shrubs are burgeoning,
and normality of a sort
will eventually re-emerge from its cocoon.
A mere facsimile
for what the confined and oppressed
would have taken to be their lot,
inmates with their infected lungs in the Gulag's frigid wastes,
the wretched of the earth the *Internationale* had once extolled.
For a brief moment,
the Gatsby set has met the lower depths.

April 15

In the Season of the Plague

In the season of the plague
a global assembly was convened
with eminent philosophers, theologians
and assorted aides-de-camp
to guide humanity through its troubles.
Sitting a full row apart from each other,
one held up a copy of *The Koran*,
with cries of *Allahu Akbar* reverberating through the hall,
another *The New Testament*,
with faint echoes of the *Matthäus Passion* as accompaniment,
an angry tribune a copy of *Das Kapital*,
abjuring the hedge funds and captains of finance,
a passionate but better dressed rival, *The Wealth of Nations*,
the salve for an economically stricken planet,
followed by a poker-faced emissary extolling *The Prince*,
along with choice bits from Kongfuzi's *Analects*,
even as a dissident freshly released
trumpeted *The Social Contract's* enduring virtues.
So the debate raged on for days,
until the assembly by now much depleted,
having reached no agreement
was finally disbanded,
and a lowly cleaner, a *Dalit* by birth,
disinfecting the cavernous halls and latrines,
scattered herbs from her village and chanted full-throated
mantras to exorcize the abominable plague.

April 18

A Litany of Plagues

The Athenian plague of 430 BC with 100,000 dead
       that did Pericles in
The Justinian plague 541–542 AD 25 to 100 million dead
       that helped do the Roman Empire in
The Bubonic plague 1347–1351
       that did 25 to 50 million Europeans in
The Cocoliziti plague — perhaps TB — 1545–1548
       that did 15 million indigenous Mexicans in
The great plague of London 1665–1666. 100,000 dead
The plague of Marseille 1720–1723. 120,000 dead
The Russian plague 1889–1890. 1 million dead
The Spanish flu 1918–1919. 20 to 50 million dead
The Asian flu 1956–1958. 1 to 3 million dead
AIDS, since 1981. 32 million dead
SARS, MERS, EBOLA — tiny numbers overall
COVID-19

Humanity has had a long-time fling
with lice, rats, marmots, pigs, and bats
and the bugs always win.

April 22

Inspired by an article and chart in *Le Point*, April 16, 2020,
"Et les puces précipitèrent la chute de l'empire romain"

Stories

"We're stories telling stories."
                    — Pessoa

In this plague-infested era
everyone has stories
from souls living by their solitary selves
to couples locked away with or without their offspring
in a variant of Sartre's hell,
to the unfortunates in shelters, tents, or sprawling shanty towns
packed by the dozen into some tiny squalid space.
And then there are the clever ones
who absconded to their well-anointed second homes,
fleeing all that was putrid, loathsome and grim.
When it will be over
journals, novels, TV and movie scripts
will be left to testify
for when the next zoonotic pathogen jumps the gun
that we were only words telling each other stories
to drive away our fears.

April 23

The Unravelling

How fortunate it must have been
to be present at new beginnings,
the end of bloody wars,
the springtime of revolution,
tumbling prison walls,
novel ways of thinking.
But there are periods of unravelling
when wars begin, crops fail,
authoritarian rule sets in,
pestilence rages,
familiar patterns of interacting with one another
begin to fall apart,
as our unhappy selves,
the ones the tragedians had warned us about,
come into their own,
and bit by bit begin to challenge
the unexamined premises of our being.

April 24

Be Kind, Be Calm, Be Safe

British Columbia has not always been
a beacon of kindness, of calmness or of safety.
One thinks of how its Indigenous peoples
were historically dealt with,
Asians at the turn of an earlier century,
Japanese Canadians during the expulsions of 1942.
One remembers the labour disputes, often bloody,
providing little quarter
for those who threatened the established order.
One recalls landslides, mining disasters,
avalanches, forest fires,
raging rivers and an oft tempestuous sea.
Yet in the 2020 pandemic
the province has been something of a standout,
its provincial officials taking science seriously,
introducing regulations expeditiously,
its population internalizing social distancing
almost as second nature,
and all together flattening the curve
more successfully than many others.

April 25

"This is our time to be kind, to be calm and to be safe."
— Dr. Bonnie Henry, B.C. Chief Health Officer, March 17, 2020

Asclepius

Son of Apollo and a mortal princess,
trained in the healing arts by Chiron the centaur,
his rod with its entwined serpent
is now the symbol of the medical profession.
Slain by Zeus
for daring to bring back the dead
from the realm of Hades — some say for lucre —
he exceeded the limits of his powers.
Still, with his shrine installed
above the Theatre of Dionysius
he presided over evocations of the plague
in *Oedipus Rex, The Women of Trachis,* or *Hippolytus.*
And his disciples to this day
pay the price for drawing too close
to the stricken and infected
when zoonotic viruses are unleashed upon the planet.

April 27

Robin Michell-Boyask, *Plague and the Athenian Imagination:*
Drama, History, and the Cult of Asclepius

What Might the Poet Have Said?

What might the Poet have said
about pandemics rolling in from the East,
port cities ravaged, galleys infested,
sailors consigned to their fate?
What might the Poet have said
about how the saga would end,
new generations stirring, old ones expiring,
as nature wreaked its revenge?
What might the Poet have said
about Eros's masks and protective attire,
not even a hint as the hours ticked by
of the passions and flames of desire?
What might the Poet have said
about the old in locked nursing homes,
no loved ones to haunt them, no mirrors to taunt them
with flashes of the youth they'd once known?

April 28

A Dystopian Tale

At first fear is universal, a great leveller,
for viruses pay no attention to ideology, social rank,
gender or religious inclination,
chipping away at the porous walls of economies, societies,
and much-vaunted civilizations.
There is solidarity of a sort
in knowing that a mere cough or touch
can spread the dreaded killer,
as social intercourse grinds to a halt
and populations hurriedly retreat
to the sanctuary of home for bare survival.
But soon enough deep fault lines come to the fore
as those possessing little succumb more quickly
than those possessing more,
as states manoeuvre to stay a step or two
ahead of their dreaded rivals,
as the spirit of *sauve-qui-peut*
once again threatens to prevail.

May 3

The Historical *Imaginaire*

Hegel with his grandiose imagination
— his critics might claim his megalomania —
wrote of world historical figures,
Alexander, Caesar, Napoleon,
who alter the course of events forever
and like emptied husks are then cast aside.
Fernand Braudel with his historical *imaginaire*
spoke of world-economies,
fanning out from the north Italian city-states,
a burgeoning 17th-century Holland,
an England on whose empire the sun would never set,
the New World colossus
which as the 21st century unfolds
may be getting its comeuppance.
And through it all
volcanoes, cyclones, and tsunamis,
droughts and torrential rainfalls,
viruses and melting icecaps
provide the changing stage props
for the human *Commedia.*

May 19

The Floral Arts

This would have been her favourite season,
assembling the assorted geraniums, pansies,
fuchsia and nasturtium,
preparing the clay or ceramic receptacles,
mixing compost, recycled earth, and potting soil
in a rusting wheelbarrow
until the backyard, the deck, the front stairs as well
were a medley to the floral arts.
You were but her assistant,
reluctant at first to take her gardening seriously,
endless visits to the nurseries,
hours of labour that by the autumn
had turned to dust.
Yet here you sit in the season of the plague
surrounded by rainbow colours
you have potted with your own hands,
certain she would have taken pleasure
in this belated homage.

May 20

In the Shadow of Pompeii

How fitting and yet ironic
that the British Museum
in the year of Brexit and the coronavirus
should mount a mammoth exhibition
sponsored by Goldman Sachs no less
on Herculaneum and Pompeii.
Is it because one senses kinship of a sort
between the fate of those twin cities
done in by their volcanic neighbour
and that of our globalized planet
struggling with a zoonotic virus?
Or that the gap between the Roman upper crust
dwelling in Pompeii's fashionable villas
and the mass of slaves ministering to their every need
recall the one percent of our own day
so far removed from the precariat and underclass
consigned to hovels?
Or can it be for fear that the verities
the western middle class had taken for granted
might incandescently turn to powder
much like in the day and night of terror
two thousand years ago
when a pyroclastic flow foretold the end of time?

May 21

The Great Reversal

Few words in the vernacular
have been more abused than "great",
the names of emperors and kings,
Charlemagne, Peter, Frederick, Catherine,
as though their deeds were beyond earthly measure,
wars like the one
meant to put an end to war itself,
proving a dismal failure in this as well,
false prophets of a bold tomorrow
like the Helmsman Mao,
hurling tens of millions forward
with a great leap into the abyss,
homunculi in more recent years
promising to make their countries great again,
and now a tiny virus,
threatening to unravel decades of global hubris
in what might well be termed the great reversal.

May 24

Checks and Balances

In the ideal republic,
quoth Polybius, Montesquieu or Madison,
power must check power.
The kingly one is too dangerous
to entrust to an unchecked figure
all too quick to trample
over both sacred and profane
with a praetorian guard at his command.
The legislative with too weak an authority in control,
can quickly overswell its banks
and divvy up within its own encrusted ranks
the spoils of office.
Judges for their part,
given too free a rein,
can use the instruments of self-interested interpretation
to impose rules
where lawmakers never deigned to venture.
A fine doctrine for fair weather times.
But when the times are rife
with strife, pestilence, and fear,
and citizens too bitter and divided
to recall the underlying need
to show a minimum of regard for one another,
how easy for the demagogue, the providential leader,
to overwhelm the forces of restraint
and impose an iron rule
from which republics cannot easily recover.

June 2

Re-reading Rilke on a Rainy Afternoon

He's like an old acquaintance
neglected with time,
in his threadbare clothes from the Paris years,
before fame had come his way,
reflecting on Judaea's prophets,
on kings who'd lost their thrones,
on courtesans with their poisoned prey,
on beggars or the mad.
Apollo's archaic torso comes to life,
Euridyce from beyond the grave,
Rodin's *atelier*, the *Orangerie*,
the panther in its cage.
And in the fevered, cloistered months
we have now entered,
his angels hover in the air,
ministers of redemption, of implacable fear.

June 3

Georg Buchner

He entered your life by chance
one sleepless night
leaving traces of his molten prose,
the hallucinations of mad Lenz,
Woyzeck's sullied honour,
Danton condemned by the Tribunal he had created,
to arouse your imagination.
Was this revolutionary adherent
of Young Germany in the 1830s,
a doctor by training, a litterateur by vocation,
a victim of typhus at the tender age of twenty-three,
the trailblazer of modern European prose
as has been claimed?
Perhaps.
But it is the saga of youthful inspiration,
unfinished novellas,
a life snuffed out almost before it had begun
that stirs you in these COVID days.

June 4

The Kindergarten Picture

The five-year-olds sit in rows,
a standing one holding up the rear,
most smiling at the camera,
some with shut eyes or distracted grimaces,
not knowing how their world will unfold.
Baby boomers before the term had been conceived,
they had many steps to take
before they might assume the roles
that life in an affluent society could provide.
How many are still alive
seventy years after the photo had been taken?
How many have had to come to terms
with the setbacks and defeats
which even the swiftest must endure?
And what of today's pandemic kids
whose virtual group photograph
will grace a century that threatens to pay the price
for the years of unchecked growth
that marked the 1950 kindergarten class?

June 6

Murmurs of a Sunday Afternoon

In this tiny park
which the surrounding campus threatens to engulf,
the sun makes its mark,
three young boys playing spy
behind the bushes and the rocks,
adults chatting on the lawn,
an Asian woman with her aged mom
seated on a nearby bench,
the bike you haven't ridden for years
at your side,
and the virus,
an unseen presence too intrusive to ignore.

June 7

A Parable

A passage in Boccaccio's *Life of Dante* has it
that some good women of Verona
seeing the poet passing by
agreed that you could tell he'd been to the Inferno
by his singed hair and dark complexion.
As we view
the unkempt locks and pale complexion
of our pandemic comrades,
we can tell the many months they've spent
in lockdown and confinement.

June 8

A Chorus of Nightingales

"The river of years has lost them."
— Borges, *To a Minor Poet of the Greek Anthology*

In evoking Theocritus and his nightingale,
Borges reminds me of an evening
twenty-five or thirty years ago,
on the beach near Agios Ioannis,
the sea calm, a sliver of moon overhead,
and in a copse of aspen
a chorus of nightingales
serenading our little company.
We have only fragments
of what the poet wrote,
like shards of pottery
or chiselled bits of marble
from where a temple to one of the Olympians
might have stood.
As for my companions of that midsummer night,
one or two have descended
the steep path towards Tartarus
and what we may have said to one another
has forever vanished.
But the nightingales and their choral song
come back to me,
as I revisit Borges's tribute
in this catastrophic year.

June 11

Chronos

> *"Democritus of Adera plucked out his eyes in order to think:*
> *Time has been my Democritus."*
> — Borges "In Praise of Darkness"

I have been spared Borges's blindness,
deafness that shuts music out,
diabetes with its oscillating sugar levels,
heart disease, renal failure, and madness worst of all.
Nor have I really known misfortune,
be it in love — though there have been oscillations,
be it in employment — mine was the lucky generation,
be it in basic human needs.
Au contraire, I have been able to indulge in travel,
before the plague set in,
in vivid intercourse with the world of letters,
in scores of fruitful friendships through the years.
But there is no escaping the fateful denouement
that time holds out for everyone.

June 14

Alone

"The flight of the alone to the Alone."
— Plotinus

What might it mean
to fly from one solitude
to an even larger Solitude?
Can solitude brook company,
is there some larger canopy
where Solitude can embrace myriads
under its wing?
Where might the game of reflecting mirrors,
the larger one containing the smaller one
down to the infinitesimal, culminate,
and can that point in turn
be the abode of the Absolute,
along with the One and the soul?
Perhaps the only alone we can ever really know
as the pandemic has underlined
is the one we carry by our side.

June 21

La Muerte

*"Death keeps watch on me
from Cordoba's towers."*
— Federico Garcia Lorca, "Rider's Song"

In the poetic *imaginaire*,
as in the artistic,
a skeletal figure lurks in the passageways
as in the high towers,
ever-present, biding his time
— why is it seldom a she? —
knowing full well its hour will come.
We die one by one,
some with horrid spasms
or entrails open to the elements,
others in the antiseptic quiet
of a hospice or a family home,
some far too early,
prey to war, pestilence or natural disaster,
others stretching their failing organs
into centenarian overtime:
This one rendez-vous we always keep.

June 23

Old Songs

Paco Ibanez in concert, Palau de la Musica,
Barcelona, 2002

To hear these songs anew,
shades of Moorish kings,
of poets doomed to exile,
of gypsies galloping in the wind,
and hopes expunged forever,
recalls heart-felt stirrings
from long ago.
Like the duende of flamenco
or the saudade of fado
these were neither tinsel tunes
nor pop songs of the hour,
gripping the listener in an era newly steeped in sorrow
with a gravity that harrows.

June 24

Of Muses

*"Are you the one whom Dante heard dictate
the lines of the Inferno?"*
— Anna Akhmatova, "The Muse"

We usually think of them
on their ethereal Olympian slopes
bathing in its coolest streams,
flying to the side of moon-struck lovers
or grief-stricken bards
mourning the dearly departed.
Yet they are no less at home
with pestilence and martial settings,
Homer with a plague
decimating the Greek contingent on Ilion's plain,
the Mahabharata
with its feuding Kaurava and Pandava princes,
Shakespeare with his bombastic celebration of Agincourt.
The muses are all too-human in their stances,
and just as cruel.

July 6

On Suicide

All these years I had failed to understand
why some would slit their wrists,
gulp down a vial of sleeping pills,
or rev the engine at a steep turn in the road.
The burden must have been too great,
the insensate feeling of life passing them by,
confined to the tiny space
they had eked out for themselves,
the dead-end job with the same dreary lot,
the broken marriage and one-night stands,
the tightening knot they felt inside
while their one or two upbeat friends
sought to cheer them up.
But now, though I'm not one to take the plunge,
I've come to sense how the sheer impossibility of soldiering on
with the pandemic in full stride
can drive the disconsolate over the edge.

July 12

On a Passage in Dante

"Rejoice, Florence, since you are so great
that you beat your wings over sea and land,
and your fame spreads throughout hell."
— *Inferno, xxvi, 1–3*

America, the beautiful,
the free, the powerful,
the most envied state on earth,
unflappable in its self-confidence,
a league or two above its would-be rivals
in technological prowess, material abundance,
in its approximation to El Dorado.
Florence had been no backwater in its day,
its commerce spreading far and wide,
its artisans justly esteemed,
its architects, painters, sculptors, literati
setting the gold standard for the Renaissance.
But the exiled Dante in visiting the Inferno
noted how many of its illustrious denizens
had ended up down there,
their self-preening the flip side of the disaster
which endless conflicts between Guelfs and Ghibellines
and factions within each could not allay.
So with America in the year of the pandemic,
its failures too conspicuous to conceal,
its racial tensions, its venal rulers,
its overweening rich
amidst a struggling underclass,
its divisions even more bitter
than Dante had ever had reason to record.

July 13

The Poor Empress

"You work on paper which is smooth, supple,
and offers no opposition to your imagination or
pen. But I, a poor empress, work on human
skin which is rather irritable and sensitive."
— Catherine the Great to Diderot

Pity the poor Empress
who must contend with human frailty
while seeking to weave, almost against nature,
a far-flung and discordant empire together.

Pity the Party Secretary
who has reason to fear
the duplicity of his rivals
and the resistance of an exhausted populace
to promises of a glorious tomorrow.

Pity Presidents and Prime Ministers
who must sacrifice their privacy
to the full glare of prying eyes
and the pursuit of personal ends
(or so they claim)
to the blandishments of power.

Pity the poor subjects
whose skin and bones so often pay the price
for what those who wield dominion over them
determine as their fate.

July 14

Adrift

Adrift somewhere between wakefulness and sleep,
first twitter of song-birds
filtering through a screen,
images of people we had never known.
How account for the myriads who have had to flee
hand-to-mouth existence in some urban slum
to thread-bare villages
where life turns on a coin,
for the brazen acts by which sociopaths
dismiss the gravity of the times,
for the spiralling loss of trust
that social distancing and forced confinement
have inflicted in their wake,
for fractured communal and family ties,
loneliness and stress,
dread of what follows when the dark dissipates
and the full blaze of morning light
reminds us there is no escape
into our childhood dreams?

July 15

'twill Always Be So

EU reaches "pivotal" coronavirus recovery deal

Another night-long foray,
masks and all,
into the cyclical Rubik's cube game
of trying to keep 27 players aligned,
the frugal North,
a Club Med in distress,
the two locomotives
of the postwar European project,
and an authoritarian-minded East.
This crisis, for all the acrimony,
the bated curses under the breath,
ended moderately well,
with a tiny hint of something new,
an element of intra-European solidarity
in the pandemic's wake.
Does it herald a messianic age
where borders further fade away
and the ghosts of visionaries of yore
— Comenius, the Abbé de St. Pierre,
Kant, Monnet —
can take a whirl or two around the ballroom floor?
Only an outsider could be so misled.
Instead, a further milestone has been set
in putting off the judgment day
the sceptics have been praying for
from the moment it all began,
when the sovereign itch proves irresistible
and a foreordained crisis proves the final one,
or as their stalwart opponents would maintain,
but one more pitfall to be overcome.

July 21

In illo tempore

"It doesn't matter if you're stupid or smart,
if you've got money or not, if you're handsome
or ugly. The earth swallows us all."
— Miguel Braga, Sao Paulo gravedigger

Some lock themselves
behind concrete walls and gardened villas,
others throwing caution to the wind,
party as though there were no tomorrow,
a few seek solace in jogging for hours,
others in yoga or stern meditation,
myriads suffer from hunger, others from gorging,
some from solitude, others from crowding,
experts declaim on the need for strict measures,
white coats compete for a miracle cure,
tensions show no signs of abetting
as infections keep surging and reprieves prove hollow,
and despite the bromides one hears from one's leaders
the gravediggers prove the wisest of all.

July 23

Five Lives

Jenny Erpenbeck, The End of Days

From the Polish plains
to the Viennese Woods
to the killing fields of the borderlands
the tale folds and unfolds.
Intermarriage that breaks the rules,
desperate times as the 7031 tram
transports cadavers from the Spanish flu
to Vienna's central burial grounds,
confessions as the Stalin trials stay true to script,
Berlin Walls that come tumbling down,
nursing homes where memory sticks to the toast and jam
and coffee stains the trembling hands of the confined.
Imagined lives that we can relive
as fate plays chess with destiny
and generations who have had it good
learn the signposts of calamity.

July 26

A Machiavellian Century

It never really vanished,
the curse of realpolitik,
the use of fraud and veiled threats,
the mailed fist against one's foes,
a witch's brew now substituting for princely rule
a patina of popular acclaim,
a nationalist refrain played to the hilt,
leaders accountable to the hoi polloi only in name.
Perhaps it was destined to be so,
the laboratory of the Renaissance opening the door
to a maze of competing experiments
that hatched the modern state
and formulae for domination following in its wake.
All is not lost, to be sure,
Machiavelli's *Discourses* evoking a republican side
that celebrates the public weal,
a balancing of contending interests
allowing liberty to prevail.
Still, two decades into this century's great game,
his princely foxes and lions are having an impressive run.

Aug. 3

Between Two Worlds

"Wandering between two worlds,
one dead, the other powerless to be born."
— Matthew Arnold, "Stanzas from the Grande Chartreuse"

Another century, yet the old lament,
the world one knows slipping away
like Alpine snows or once fertile plains
where a desiccated scirocco now blows.
As for the unknown,
one senses the promises of ever bolder,
sager chapters still to come,
are so much candy floss
to a pandemic world frozen in its tracks.
Some may hunker down
to a faith they never left,
to feasts, fasts, and endless prayers
to a deity that has yet to show its face.
Others may remain convinced
technology with its multiple apps,
will extricate us one more time
from obstacles that bar our path.
But for those who struggle
with the blighted vestiges of hope,
there is a gnawing sense
that happy endings are best reserved for fairy tales.

Aug. 5

Eris

The goddess of strife and discord,
uninvited guest at the marriage of Peleus and Thetis,
she threw the golden apple amidst the goddesses
that set the Trojan War in motion.
Her numerous offspring numbered pain, starvation, hardship,
battles, war, mass slaughter,
lies, forgetfulness and ruin,
no small feat for one mere goddess.
She was to show her mark
on multiple occasions,
long after the fame and glory of Olympus
had been extinguished.
Even today she casts her spell
as mortals flounder in the pandemic's shadow,
old against young,
the masked against inveterate foes of masking,
the sheltered in their bubbles vs. the wretched souls
who must clean up the mess,
with nary a fellow god or goddess
to provide solace.

Aug. 8

The Intruder

"Think of life as a novel . . . After a certain point
it's not a good idea to introduce a new major character."
— Salman Rushdie, *The Golden House*

Societies are not all that different.
They too expect consistency,
a proper evolution from points A to B to C,
some kind of demographic balance,
adequate rainfall, temperature range,
immigration flows, economic projections.
So when a new element is introduced,
holus-bolus into the equation,
like an unexpected guest at a family celebration
or old-timers' reunion,
it upends the apple-cart.
Suddenly we need to reconfigure our lexicon
— confinement, social distancing,
flattening the curve, masks and ventilators —
none too happy about an intruder
disrupting familiar patterns of behaviour.

Aug. 10

To Unseat a Tyrant

for Svetlana Tikhanovskaya

What courage the women of Belarus have shown,
first the horrors of the war,
then Chernobyl's gruesome rain,
then that forceful journalist, Svetlana Alexievich,
unwilling to leave a single stone from the Soviet era unturned,
and now another Svetlana stepping in
during this summer's pandemic,
when her husband had been whisked away,
to speak the simple truth
cherished by all who suffer under an iron boot,
the right to breathe, to speak,
to have a government responsive to basic needs,
this with cynicism the tyrant's calling card.

Aug. 11

Keeping Score

The numbers keep leapfrogging by a quarter million,
as though the spores had decided
to play team tag with each other.
Sometimes it is holiday-makers
returning from their southern jaunts,
sometimes clusters of young people,
drinking, raving, craving company
as raging hormones egg them on,
sometimes family gatherings,
market transactions in close quarters,
cramped public transportation,
or the serendipity of simply breathing.
Many are afraid,
others fearless in their disdain
for masks or social distancing,
for an irksome virus that dares to challenge
their aptitude for sheer endurance.
Soon summer will turn to autumn,
and magical thinking about vaccines
to wipe the scoreboard clean
prove one more milestone
as the pandemic keeps one step ahead.

Aug. 12

A Global Age

"Crafty inventions, subtle beyond believing,
now onto evil bring them, now onto good."
— Antigone, *364–65*

It seemed a global age had dawned,
consumer goods to adorn the shopping malls,
connectivity reducing the barriers of space and time,
air travel for a song, exotic holidays,
and the dreams of a burgeoning middle class fulfilled.

The multinationals had proven more powerful than states,
wooing politicos with the glitter of high tech,
promises of jobs in droves,
and tax havens with their pots of gold.

Journalists and academics, the paparazzi of the age,
made the rounds of global entrepôts,
touting a fail-proof economic model,
a self-perpetuating motion machine,
destined, in the ripeness of time,
to lift even *les misérables* from the planetary slums.

Like a Sunday sermon to the faithful,
this discourse became the mantra of a generation.

Yet nature had a trick or two in store,
ice sheets melting in the polar north and south,
the atmosphere heating at an exponential rate,
ever fiercer tornadoes, floods, desertification, droughts,
with zoonotic interlopers to grind things to a halt.

Only for a finite period, to be sure,
for the game would inevitably resume,
the intrepid lifting themselves off the ground
as they had always done,
convinced that they could put the lie
to doomsayers of old
warning that grandiose ambition
can herald an ignominious fall.

Aug. 15

The Poisoners

History has had no shortage of famous poisoners,
Olympia, wife of Philip of Macedon
and mother to Alexander,
Candia, one of Nero's favourites
in disposing of troublesome rivals,
Lucrezia Borgia, scion of a glorious Renaissance line.
But with a former KGB Lieutenant-Colonel in charge,
the Russians have brought perfection to the art.
Alexander Litvinenko,
done in with radioactive polonium in 2006,
Sergei and Yulia Skripal, in 2012,
victims of Novichok,
a nerve agent that hinders breathing,
and now, Alexei Navalny,
in a deep coma from which he will struggle to recover.
No fingerprints point as yet to the Kremlin's spires,
only coincidences that serve to warn others
to be en garde.

Aug. 21

The Deserted Campus

"Far, far away, thy children leave the land.
Ill fares the land, to hastening ills a prey."
— Oliver Goldsmith, *The Deserted Village*

The campus where you spent your adult years
is strangely silent,
malls deserted,
buildings largely closed to human contact.
The knowledge economy,
pivot to a brave new world,
has fallen on bleak times,
hollowed out like villages of yore
or smokestack towns
where factories once held sway.
Here and there a masked passerby,
a skittery library clerk,
advancing a volume over a sterilized table top
like some purloined treasure from the deep.
Row on row of classroom desks sit empty,
with darkened overheads,
the noisy banter signalling a lecture's end
not soon to be repeated.
Such is the state of things, in year one of the pandemic,
the alma mater which its denizens held dear
a mothballed amphitheatre
with a chorus of ghostly refugees from yesteryear.

Sept. 4

Generations

A trope reaching back millennia on end,
Biblical lines stemming from Noah or from Abraham,
the Houses of Atreus or Labdacus in Greek tales,
Imperial lines and royal ones,
mercantile ones like the Hanseatic League,
and closer to home the Lost Generation,
the Depression Generation, the Greatest Generation,
the Boomers and their aftermath,
Xers, Millennials, and now the Pandemonials,
each with its own lived history, shared ethos,
and shattered dreams.

Sept. 6

Smoke and Ladders

The west coast states are a tinderbox,
the Sierras laced in smoke and flames,
stranded hikers lifted out
for threat to life and limb.
Smoke seeps into the Lower Mainland,
air quality slowly sinking,
even as the COVID index curves
in the wrong direction.
Others have it worse, much worse,
the Moria holding camp on Lesbos a total write-off,
its cramped and desperate asylum-seekers
caught between the ashes, the virus,
and the ire of islanders who have had enough.
So unfolds month seven of the pandemic.

Sept. 9

Armageddon

The fires began around New Year's Day,
this double-twenty year,
driving marsupials, sulphur-crested cockatoos,
and reptiles in their legions to extinction.
Then came the plague,
an episodic visitor from the fabled East,
spreading its wings along the new silk routes
linking global entrepôts to one another,
taking sustenance from nursing homes and market squares,
industrial hubs and far-flung villages,
leaving few corners of the earth untouched.
Next torrential floods along the Bengali plain,
fires burning up the Westcoast of a once mighty USA,
reduced like all the would-be hegemons of yore
to a bit part in an even larger scheme
nature may have in store.
Somewhere in the shadows
Gog girds on his sword,
Magog adjusts his armour and mailed vest,
as the battle of all battles, to cite an ancient text,
waits to be unleashed.
Not bad for a mere pimple of a hill,
Har Megiddo,
near the Valley of Jezreel in ancient Israel,
back again to play a leading role.

Sept. 12

Nuclear Winter

The toll of the pandemic-stricken keeps ticking upwards,
sprinting past the thirty million mark,
and now carbonized particles
from our neighbour's conflagration
have turned the landscape outside our windows grey,
crowding out all vestiges of summer.
Perhaps it had to be this way,
successive blows from a nature *furiosa*,
unleashing floods, locusts, cyclones and infernal fires,
informing us it has had enough.
Or is it only in our febrile imaginations
that we sense the cup is overflowing,
that even acts of atonement and contrition
would be like howling in a storm.

Sept. 15

Shedding

Slowly we have learned to shed
simple verities we took for granted,
easy intercourse with strangers, friends
now that the very air has become a lethal conduit,
venues where we had turned for simple satisfactions —
restaurants, bars, gyms, cinemas or sports arenas —
the work place with its endless bustle,
subway lines, airport hubs,
vacation getaways, family celebrations.
We have come to face
new trials and tribulations,
clouds of locusts,
wildfires of surreal proportions,
surging seas with cyclone after cyclone,
diluvial downpours from the pages of *Gilgamesh.*
Peeling away layer after layer,
we have discovered how little we had progressed
from civilization's earlier foundations,
from the Cro-Magnons who had preceded us,
from when sheer survival as a species
sweeps away all sundry preoccupations.

Sept. 16

Jewish New Year 2020/5781

Memories of when this date
marked the start of the High Holidays
with brisk autumn air and scarlet maple leaves
welcome emissaries from some higher sphere.
The house was festive with foodstuffs and decor,
and the synagogue a place of earnest prayer
and fervent conversation
within the micro-world of my *coreligionnaires.*
So far away the spirit of those days,
a faith long since abandoned,
vanished like those who nurtured me
in my formative, childhood stage.
I have little desire to revisit
the hidden god of Auschwitz and Mauthausen
whose unsettled accounts
with the ash and bitter tears of the victims
reached to the heavens.
But for those who died
and loved ones who have since then disappeared
I mark this day as one of recollection
in this grim pandemic year.

Sept. 17

The Tenses

The past could be nearer,
the present more endearing,
the future less dismal than appears.

Sept. 22

Poem in a Minor Key

Sadness builds on days like this,
rain on concrete, rain on grass,
water leaching from the leaves
that soon will disappear.
Something rankles deep within,
promises you never made,
debts incurred for faults
that weren't even yours.
That's the rub as the pandemic sets in
and there's time to brood
over dozens of things past,
feeling guilt for still being alive
and in half decent shape to boot
when others are rudderless or lost.

Sept. 23

The Second Wave

It was tough enough adjusting
to incessant calls to wash your hands with soap,
avoid touching your face,
remember to mask up,
stay as far away from strangers in your path
as safe distancing dictates,
work from inside your domicile when possible,
help your kids negotiate
the ersatz classes on the screen,
and keep your sanity intact.
Now comes a second wave,
perhaps less lethal than the first, perhaps not,
where congregating together, eating out in groups,
rallying in numbers for some cause,
praying communally to some god,
are once again taboo.
This time the young, or young at heart,
are designated as the carrier group,
as overstretched hospitals and staff
prepare for yet another round of testing sites,
improvised wards and ICUs,
the mood out there darkening with the autumn sky
as folks who thought the virus was a one-season pest
learn that visitors like this
have come to call our species home.

Sept. 25

One Million

"The death of one man is a tragedy.
The death of millions is a statistic."
—Joseph Stalin

COVID-19 has passed the official one million mark,
though we know it is a good deal higher,
for statistics are lacking or suppressed in scores of countries,
and many who die outside of hospitals and nursing homes
will not be properly reported.
Those who have lost a loved one
can pin a face, a life story,
a tragic turn of fate,
to their disappearance.
As for the millions who may be lost
in the carnage still underway
— the little father of the people
was an expert in such matters —
we struggle to think of them
as more than a statistic,
given the challenge to our fettered human brains
to grasp the full significance of seven digit numbers.

Sept. 29

The Fallen

Once they have crossed
the large divide
beyond the pastured fields,
the forests with their soaring masts,
the buffeted waves,
the chalk grey cliffs
to the dark lands,
no plague will intrude,
no unremitting stress,
no festive touch,
no banter of friends
to recall the past.

Sept. 30

Masks

The uninvited stranger masked in red,
crashing a survivalist hideaway
in Poe's macabre rendering,
Verdi's masked ball,
where jealous rivalry
does in a reigning king,
a geriatric on a Kyoto bus,
spine contorted,
face protected from any hostile gaze,
Halloween revelry
as squealing kids, suitably disguised,
weave their way
up and down toffee-dappled streets,
and now a universal presence,
bedecking rich and poor alike
in one bold planetary sweep.

Oct. 1

States of Consciousness

Sometimes your best lines come
when lying in bed,
suspended between wakefulness
and a state of consciousness that trips you up,
as a minefield of images and random coincidences
impress themselves on your brain,
too fleeting to pin down,
too far removed from the day's preoccupations
for you to fully understand,
as you try to follow wherever they may lead,
fearful you will lose the thread,
much like those in the larger world out there
trying to come to terms with the altered normality
the pandemic has imposed,
harking back to where things were before,
only to be forced time and time again
to acknowledge that their lives have been derailed.

Oct. 6

Hermit Crabs

You must catch the October sun between 10 and 2,
before it begins to wane
as fog descends on the beach once again
and a breeze off the sea
sends shivers through the spine,
forcing you to hurry along.
For if temperatures are surprisingly mellow
for this time of the year,
you sense this is but a side effect
of climate change,
even as the virus continues to eat away
at familiar things,
turning us into hermit crabs,
self-absorbed within our shells.

Oct. 7

The Prophets of Yore

We miss them,
those prophets with robes and deep voices,
presaging the doom that clearly awaits us,
the foe from afar who will scourge us and purge us
of sins we've committed and ruinous behaviour,
as the natural order dissolves all around us.
We yearn for the hope
that a voice from the desert
will lift up our spirits and speak of the hilltops
where sunlight is breaking
and the cycle of plagues and wanton destruction
can finally cease.
And we know that their message,
though stark could ring hollow,
and the god they bespoke
has been silenced forever,
yet we yearn for the comfort
of words of atonement
that only those who have wrestled with torment
can ever pronounce.

Oct. 12

M

You wake as the infection rate or R
ticks up another notch,
even as the morale index or M
continues to collapse.

Oct. 16

The Horror, the Horror

for Samuel Paty

Like a scene out of the Reign of Terror,
a decapitation in broad daylight
in a quiet suburban town
of a high school teacher who had dared to show
a caricature of the prophet Mohammed
as part of a classroom discussion of free speech
in what passes for a secular republic.
Knowing what had preceded
— the Charlie Hebdo massacre,
the rampages of ISIS and its associates
through Africa and the Fertile Crescent,
9/11 and its aftermath —
should we be in shock?
Intolerance seems to be the mantra of our era,
not only of the religious sort,
but political, ethnic, and racial as well,
and one more martyr
will do little to stem the horror.

Oct. 17

The Angel of Annihilation

In the midst of COVID's second wave,
geopolitics that never takes a break,
Nagorno-Karabakh,
where hundreds have been ferried to their graves
with more to follow,
Turkey abetting its Azeri ally,
as drones scatter bloodshed from the sky,
Ladakh, where the two mastodons of Asia
duke it out for bits of lunar landscape
in the high plateau,
Yemen, an enduring hell-hole,
failed states, narco-states
strewn throughout the global South,
and over it all the angel of annihilation
to cheer humanity on its way.

Oct. 18

The Stoic

There comes a time
when there is no here, no there, no anywhere
for the one who writes these lines.
And the afterlife of words like these
can prove no more enduring
than words as yet unwritten.
Mordant reflections that Marcus Aurelius
has bequeathed us.

Oct. 20

Denialism

It's comfortable in your sitting room
in these early hours,
maroon recliner, leather ottoman,
books and magazines gentle reminders
of the baggage you've acquired.
That the world out there
is coming apart at the seams
goes without say
as the virus enjoys a rejuvenated second round,
as the anger of one portion of the confined
spills over into conspiratorial chants,
sorcerers' apprentices eagerly egging them on,
until the political stage grows rancorous with discontent.

Oct. 22

Breviaries

Eight densely packed pages
Polyidos, Dolon,
Thoas and Mydon,
a tenebrous breviary
of the war's fallen soldiers.
Covid victims
of varying age and description,
Armstrong, Cordero, Loft, and Nguyen,
from the Canadian contingent
that earth has swallowed.

Oct. 29

Alice Oswald, *Memorial,* a long poem inspired by *The Iliad;* CTV News, "Remembering Canadians who have died from COVID-19."

Nov. 3, 2020

The elements of tragedy were perfectly aligned,
rival camps in a parallel universe,
a central character whose hubris
threatened to bring the pillars crashing down,
and in the background pandemic, economic meltdown,
mega-dreams and mega-nightmares
in locked embrace.
The play threatened to end badly,
for even before the first act had begun
one sensed the big divide would carry on
long after the principals had left the stage,
faith in one's just cause however flawed,
monologues now that dialogue had lost its voice,
a call to resist when votes did not add up
to the numbers that one had expected.

Nov. 3

The Morning After

Nothing has been resolved
yet everything is even clearer
than before.
What remains divided
cannot be united
come what may.
The sun may shine as brightly as before,
but Cain and Abel
will battle on.

Nov. 4

Pandemics

For leaders right and left
we are at war with a pandemic
which unchecked would put our hallowed civilization
— GDP, consumer goods, jobs,
health care and vaunted pension plans —
into meltdown mode.
And well it might,
for who but a few Cassandras on the battlements
might have foretold
what zoonotic transfers might unleash?
What of the other kinds of war,
the ones that marked the century now passed,
with their mangled corpses in the muddy fields,
their incarcerated bodies,
their starving masses and burned-out towns
or closer to our age
the civil wars that rage
from the sands of the Sahel to the Afghani hills?
And what of the lies
with which puppet-masters
with their fake blond hair,
Presidents for life,
would-be Sultans from yesteryear
hold populations in their sway?
So many pandemics to endure.

Nov. 5

Fifty Million

A new milestone has been set
as the world-wide infection rate
competes with that of pandemics past.
The death rate is far less,
at least by the official count,
but with pavements strewn with mounds of leaves
and Arctic winds blowing through the trees,
the toll can only rise.
We have lost a sense
of what normality is all about,
of how to cope with the endless isolation
the virus has decreed,
masked though many have become,
cautious in venturing out,
immured within four walls.
Those with faith in a Creator,
can implore their deity for relief;
those given to braggadocio may tough it out,
scorning the feeble in mind and body;
but those who take ill omens to heart
can only dread what winter brings.

Nov. 8

Factoid

Scores dead and missing,
over 200,000 evacuated from their homes
in Nicaragua, Honduras, and Guatemala
as Hurricane Eta strikes,
with a second storm on its way;
dozens dead in the Philippines,
more than 350,000 evacuated,
270,000 homes destroyed by typhoons;
and how many confined to the shelter of their homes,
as a second COVID wave takes hold in the global north,
bristle and complain?

Nov. 12

Nov. 13, 2020

Friday the 13th,
an inauspicious calendar day,
heralding disaster on every front.
As though we haven't had our share,
this *annus horribilis,*
the Austral bush to set it off,
the plague — a tiny far-off blip when it began —
escalating to pandemic size on a global scale,
an election in the neighbourhood
with enough drama
to keep one in perpetual suspense.
Yet somehow I take comfort on this very day.
The numbers are well enough aligned
to ensure a due transfer of power in the end,
however much the demagogue and his enablers bray.
The sound of mandolins on the radio
as I sip my tea.
evoking Vivaldi's Venice
and tales of plagues that ultimately fade.
And the biscuit à la Proust I dip into my cup
summoning up memories of happier days,
of why life, despite its treacheries,
remains the greatest gift we can receive.

Nov. 13

Soumitra Chatterjee

Dead at eighty-five,
a victim of COVID-19 like so many more,
lead actor in *The World of Apu*,
and long-time protege of Satyajit Ray.
A playwright and poet in his own right,
epitome of the Bengali intellectual,
of an openness, a restlessness
that bespoke no Bollywood acolyte
or camp follower of his country's surging Hindutva tide,
a throwback to a time
when still an adolescent
you set your own sights on a canvas
larger than your ghettoized Montreal home,
resonating to Apu's venture
as though it could some day be your own.

Nov. 15

The Burden

"To escape from the burden of freedom
into new dependencies and submission."
— Erich Fromm, *Escape from Freedom*

One may wonder why so many
would submit to the whims
and edicts of a magus
risen from the subterranean depths?
That the world is confusing
and evolving by the hour,
the bounds of things unknown
expanding behind measure,
cataclysms bearing down,
strengthen the call for an authoritarian figure
to lift the impossible burden.
And the vacuum will be filled,
if that's the express desire
of a multitude seeking absolution from the trauma
of seeking a more empowering pathway
through the torrent.

Nov. 16

Jeremiads

"The age is now senile . . . the springs have less
freshness and the autumns less fecundity . . .
a decrease of honesty in the marketplace,
of justice in court."
— Cyprian, Christian writer, 3rd century AD

Heralds of decline
have not been lacking through the ages,
looking to darkening skies, desiccated fields,
a rumbling sound from deep within the earth,
moral collapse to mark the end of time.
An opposing chorus to the one
which has accompanied Western man
— to use an old-fashioned term —
for three centuries or more,
the promise of challenging frontiers to explore,
new technologies bursting on the scene,
the arrow of progress spelling abundance
even for those who had always known none.
We are free to choose
which discourse better suits our temperament,
rosy predictions of what the future holds
or the doom and gloom of the Savonarolas of old.
Still, in periods of pandemic,
even optimists have been known
to lie low.

Nov. 21

The Year of the Four Emperors

for Yolande Grisé

Trump has sometimes been compared
to a Roman emperor,
a Caligula perhaps,
known for opposing limitations to his imperial power
during his four-year reign,
or a Nero,
though the latter was more into playing thespian or minstrel
than endless games of golf.
Nero, not unpopular with the masses,
but having executed any who opposed him,
(they call it revolving doors in Washington),
was himself forced to commit suicide
once the armies had had enough.
This opened the door to a year of great instability, 69AD,
four emperors in a row,
Galba, Otho, Vitellius, and Vespasian,
the first and third done in by the Praetorian Guard,
the second driven to suicide,
until the fourth managed to restore order to the realm.
A useful bit of history to recall,
as a new game of thrones unfolds
in the pandemic's shadow.

Nov. 22

A New Credo

In the 19th century
nihilists questioned the underlying premises
of the prevailing social order.
The 20th century saw ideologies in the saddle,
fascism in tooth and claw,
communism at its most intransigent,
nationalism, both moderate and extreme,
shoring up the middle.
Now the 21st century sees a new credo in the ascendant
— denialism.
Holocausts never happened,
Gulags a dissident insinuation,
the Great Leap Forward or madness of the Cultural Revolution
an irrelevant aberration,
electoral defeat by any normal measure
figments of one's opponents' imagination.
And to cap it off,
rising sea levels, melting ice floes,
raging cyclones and pandemics
relegated to the realm of science fiction.

Nov. 23

Nostalgia

"It was different in those days . . .
Every stone lay in its place.
The streets of life were decently paved."
— Joseph Roth, *The Radetsky March*

Oh those halcyon days
when we were young,
when order reigned,
and the corners of despair
had not yet turned our worlds upside down.
An old refrain,
each generation as it ages
harking back with some exaggeration
to a simpler, more fulfilling time.
Such was the elongated summer of peace
that had held Europe in its sway
before the dam would finally burst.
Such the memories of abandoned homes
where refugees in bare bones tents and corrugated huts
now scrounge for their existence.
Such too the laments
of baby-boomers in their cups,
or millennials recalling the ease
with which new futures could be summoned up,
as they contemplate the havoc
COVID in nine short months has wrought.

Nov. 24

The Winter of our Discontent

Well into a second wave,
even before the serious frost and snow descend,
and the time we're forced to spend indoors
becomes an incubator for what's close at hand.
The virus is mutating,
its spike protein better adapted to scaling
whatever defences our antibodies may throw up,
vaccines be damned.
The *vox populi* cries out for closure
— the same was true the first winter of the Great War —
but the band of COVID spreaders
marches merrily on.
The drumbeat to see this mega-nightmare through
has just begun.

Nov. 28

The Daemons

"We have become rich in knowledge,
but poor in wisdom."

— Carl Jung

How easily we mistake
scientific breakthroughs, technological prowess,
economic suppleness, political craftiness,
literary showmanship, artistic exuberance,
for some qualitative leap forward for our species.
Warfare is as endemic as before,
inequality just as rampant,
pandemics no less a fact of life
than floods or famine.
Yet somehow we persist in thinking
we are smarter at the age-old game
of trying to coexist with one another
while keeping the dark daemons at bay.

Nov. 28

The Ancients

We scorn the ancients at our own expense,
confident that ours is a vastly superior civilization,
with its industrial heft, technological prowess,
material abundance,
beggaring all that had preceded.
There are many more of us
on this beleaguered planet,
of every race, tribe, and ethnic description,
and the common lot,
at least in the more privileged corners of the globe,
has attained a living standard
that the helots or plebes of old
would well have envied.
But the ancients knew that hubris
— in great empires as in petty city-states —
came at a price,
that wars and plagues and civil discontents
were not one-off events
but part and parcel of the human disposition,
that what had once occurred
could haunt our future days.
We scorn the ancients at no small expense.

Nov. 29

The World of Yesterday

"The nineteenth century was honestly convinced
that it was on the straight and unfailing path
toward being the best of all worlds."
— Stefan Zweig, *The World of Yesterday*

Stefan Zweig wrote with an exile's deep chagrin
of the language he had lost to barbarism,
of a civilization which had wrought enormous feats
now in ruins.
We do not face as dark a moment
— the pandemic for all its devastation
is not a world war —
yet we sense amidst the roll-call of the stricken
that the life we took for granted
partakes in ways still difficult to contemplate
of yesterday.

Nov. 30

The Fog of War

The high command barks its orders
but in the rear they hear what they want to hear
as orderlies are swept off their feet,
weeks without sleep,
the infected and the corpses piling up in makeshift trenches,
with field hospitals overwhelmed.
Rumours abound,
as they always do in times like this,
an armistice is in the works,
the enemy sufficiently depleted to sue for peace.
For others,
a second and third wave is underway,
as reinforcements swell the breach
the enemy's spring offensive had unleashed.
Amidst the confusion whom should one believe,
those convinced the war is drawing to a close,
or those barricading themselves far behind the lines
in angst at what the coming months may bring?

Dec. 5

Just Asking

The thrust to remake our mode of thinking,
our urban spaces,
to harness nature's power in unanticipated ways,
is undiminished,
for this pandemic is a mere hiccup
in the endless quest
to keep the Faustian bargain intact.
It has served us well,
since the scientific breakthroughs of centuries ago,
the dawning of the Industrial Revolution,
the age of steel, of concrete and of glass,
of flight, container vessels,
and the Internet.
So why assume like the Nostradamuses of our era
an inevitable end to the joy ride
the better endowed portion of the planet
has taken to be its right?
Even if the fates
have some kind of *Dämmerung* in store
for our cheeky species,
would it alter our programmed behaviour one iota?
Just asking.

Dec. 9

Dualities

"His mask which is now lifeless . . .
is tender and open to the air."
— Rainer Maria Rilke, "Death of the Poet"

The masks we wear
as grim acknowledgement
of the intrepid visitor at our door
have become a badge of endurance
in battling our age-old foe.
Quite unlike the masks
the dying slip on
in bidding their farewell.

Dec. 11

California North

B.C. has long been this country's California,
as far West as one could go,
the place where life for many could begin anew,
where gold panners and lumberjacks,
remittance men and "Orientals"
— to recall a demeaning term from the past —
could interface,
with fortunes to be easily made and lost,
and in more recent times,
with migrants continuing to pour in
and high-tech jobs increasingly the norm,
sexual practices, drug laws,
and religious observance more relaxed.

The pandemic heralds a different lesson of sorts.
California has suffered 1.3 million cases to date,
25 thousand new infections a day,
20,000 deaths and counting.
B.C., with one-eighth the population,
has had 40,000 cases to date,
some 750 new infections per day,
600 deaths and counting.

Is it pragmatic common sense
that has made us more fastidious
in the mask wearing and social distancing
our health authorities
have been cajoling us to embrace?
Is our population mix:
far fewer Latinos or Blacks,
a higher Asian component,
the differentiating factor?
Or is it a residue of Old World values
coupled with a dose of Lady Luck
that have kept us on a straighter, narrower path?

Dec. 12

Bach

In troubled times
we take what comfort we can
from forest canopy and rugged peaks,
murmuring waves, a shoreline by the sea,
chromatic music from a less complicated age.

Dec. 13

The Frankfurt School

"History as a permanent catastrophe."
— Theodore Adorno

As you read some passages from the Frankfurt School,
on the grim view these exiles from Nazi Germany
came to hold on the legacy of the Enlightenment,
on the place of progress in the Western *imaginaire*,
on our domination over nature
or the reduction of culture
to a mere accoutrement of material accumulation,
you sense the irony.
Caught up in a quite different catastrophe,
we are suddenly conscious that the foundations
of our own belief in upwards, ever upwards,
in technology as the magic key
to an ever-expansive economic project,
in the inevitable victory
of the more generous over the more sinister impulses
in human nature
may have been a mirage,
blinding us to forces that can quickly turn
Sunday afternoon in a crowd
into a premonition of disaster.

Dec. 14

Numbers

"Take ye the sum of all the congregation
of the children of Israel."
                               — Numbers, *I.ii*

For census takers a tool of the trade,
keeping pace with shifting currents
in the demographic sweepstakes
that keep nation-states afloat.
For speculators,
a tool for appraising the state of play
of futures markets, currency exchange,
and more subtle indicators
of where the winds of change are blowing.
As for pandemic watchers,
as daily infection rates exceed half a million world-wide,
death rates tagging gamely along,
with the future toll of those affected in the hundred millions,
a game of numbers as sombre as they come.

Dec. 16

Through a Looking Glass

Back then,
when we could greet each other
with a friendly gesture or an embrace,
engage in conversation face to face,
not have to give a second thought
to droplets in the air that might do us in
or set us back for weeks and months,
we were blissfully unaware a time might come
when to interact would take place behind a mask
if peradventure we found ourselves in a common space,
but just as frequently through a looking glass,
in a parallel universe
where things were never quite the same.

Dec. 17

By Way of a Eulogy

for Leo Panitch

"The day of his death was a dark cold day."
— W. H. Auden, "In Memory of W. B. Yeats"

The lights are going out for a generation,
one that tried to infuse this sleepy country
with its habit of playing second fiddle
to Uncle Sam,
to try to carve out a different course
in its foreign policy, its political economy,
its underlying raison d'être.
With some limited successes, here and there,
where draft dodgers from the Vietnam War were concerned,
or dissent from the second Iraqi War,
with a modestly egalitarian turn in health care,
gender relations, and social policy at large,
with a more committed thrust
in an academy where hewing to the middle of the road
had always been the norm.
One by one they disappear,
Mel Watkins, stalwart foe of a branch plant mentality,
Jim Laxer, his co-combatant for a Canada on the left,
and now Leo, felled by COVID,
faithful to the old Marxist mole to his very last.
In this pandemic year,
death has lost the ability to shock
and eulogies the power to lift our hearts.
But mourn we must,
our confrères who have passed away.

Dec. 20

Crises

Crises have a way
of forcing us to come to terms
with paradoxes we ignore,
that others have it so much worse
and our paltry claims for more
seem petty in the balance,
that our cohort has a finite moment on this planet,
like those that came before
and ones to follow,
that we must seek contentment where we can,
in love and friendship that endures,
in what nature can distill,
in the pure silence of our contemplative hours.

Dec. 21

The Unknown Masterpiece

You stumble upon Balzac's short story
quite by chance,
a 17th-century *atelier* with a young Nicolas Poussin
and an aged perfectionist/illusionist
whose painting of perfect female beauty
is but a maze of lines and colours
strangely predictive of the abstract art
of another age.
This unknown masterpiece will be destroyed
and its creator perish in a single night.
In a year when culture with a capital "C"
has been under permanent assault,
many a creator and masterpiece
will suffer a similar fate.

Dec. 22

The Gender Game

Men, we are told, not incorrectly,
have tended to dominate the social hierarchy,
sheer brawn and testosterone-driven will
flattening whatever obstacles might bar their path.
But when it comes to longevity,
theirs turns out to be the weaker sex,
XY proving more fickle a chromosome pair
than XX.
Sure enough, as the pandemic unfolds,
men are falling by the wayside in larger droves
than their female counterparts,
3-2 or 2-1 — the ratios vary.
Where long haulers are concerned,
with symptoms like fatigue, shortness of breath,
brain fog, exercise intolerance,
the proportions are reversed.
A stronger immune system
can be a weakness in the end,
provoking through vigorous attacks on the invading virus
autoimmune disease instead.
On the COVID battlefield,
neither gender really wins.

Dec. 23

Yuletide 2020

The magic of festive days
seen through the keen eyes of a child,
Fanny and Alexander's opening scenes
candles blazing, table set,
a smorgasbord, an endless feast
of toasts and songs
and dancing through the house.
All this as millions celebrate in lockdown mode,
one by one and two by two,
fearful of what the season brings
and what the new year has in store.

Dec. 25

Boxing Day

Traditionally, when poor boxes were opened
and alms were distributed to the poor,
but not in this pandemic year,
as vaccines begin to offer hope
of an exit from the drudgery
and a new reality.
With the wealthy countries of the North
having secured the lion's share
of what Big Pharma can provide,
the bottom tier of states
may have to wait till '23 or '24
for whatever alms can come their way.

Dec. 26

Pavane for a Year Now Ending

As pestilence emerged from the lower depths
where it had long resided,
silhouettes rehearsed a macabre dance
beneath a memento mori,
and we slowly withdrew from the dancing floor
to months of forced confinement
within the borders of our walls
and our restless, unhinged minds.
But dance we will and dance we must
as the clock ticks down the hours,
and we hope
— even those whose faith has lapsed —
that an *annus* less *horribilis*
will see off the one that expires.

Dec. 31

ABOUT THE AUTHOR

Philip Resnick was born in Montreal and pursued his university education at McGill, in Paris, and at the University of Toronto. For over forty years he was a member of the Department of Political Science at the University of British Columbia. His interests as a political scientist ranged widely, from Canadian politics and political economy to comparative nationalism and democratic theory. He has published extensively on these topics. He is also a published poet, who began to write poetry in his adolescence and came to pursue this interest, following his marriage to Andromache who was Greek, over the many summers he and his family came to spend in Thessaly, in the city of Volos, and in a village and cove on adjacent Mount Pelion. He makes his home in Vancouver, British Columbia.